JMJ ✝

x. Kamil J. Belling
"Ad maiorem Dei gloriam"

← *Suffer with purpose!
← *Shedding of redemptive tears!
← *In temptations we' all are tested!
← *Determination to learn with the unity of the H. spirit!
← *Sense of Sin
← *Love of God and understand of man

Keep the words of life in heart...

＊ You can't escape reality!!!

＊We have to be like Christ

＊ In suffering is joy

＊ Be glad even in sorrow (power of tears)

Vocation is necessary for today

＊ Tears in private joy in public

＊ Ordinary crosses are not extraordinary
Don't look for crosses they're around you!

Lidersheep of love... Charity
silence — to be able to truly grap
what someone give..
← secret →

sensitive, not deceptive

Selfe...

D1590989

Marygrove
EX LIBRIS

Sequen...

Love
silence
cross
suffering
secret

- not bein passive, but active
* active
- find the key... bring the best or due to occasp.

Augustin Leger...

Man to be thee

"don't you say that you love them, but
just show them that you love them!
St. John Bosco

The Church
of the Churches
The Lateran

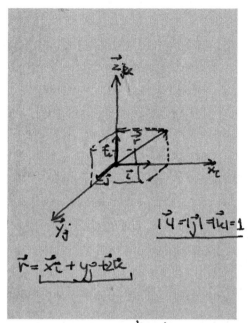

$$|\vec{i}| = |\vec{j}| = |\vec{k}| = 1$$

$$\vec{r} = x\hat{\imath} + y\hat{\jmath} + z\hat{k}$$

Be generous with this what
you have... be patient and
humble ⟶

EVE
AND THE
GRYPHON

by

GERALD VANN, O.P.

BLACKFRIARS PUBLICATIONS
OXFORD
1947

Nihil Obstat:
  Thomas E. Bird, D.D., PH.D.

Imprimatur:
  ✠ Humphrey Bright
              Vicarius Capitularis
        Birmingamiae, die 5a Junii, anno 1946.

Approbatio Ordinis:
  Nihil Obstat:
      Fr. Egbertus Cole, O.P., S.T.L.
      Fr. Ivo Thomas, O.P., S.T.L., M.A.
  Imprimatur:
      Fr. Benedictus O'Driscoll, O.P.
                        Prior Provincialis
          Londoni, die 28 Octobris, 1944.

FRONTISPIECE

THE reproduction at the beginning of this book is from a painting by El Greco. The picture is usually described as 'The Virgin'. But the owner, Mrs. Tomas Harris, considers that it is more likely to be a portrait of a young woman, possibly El Greco's own daughter, painted with his characteristic mysticism.

The author and the publishers wish to express their gratitude to Mrs. Tomas Harris for permission to reproduce the picture and also for the information cited above.

PRINTED IN GREAT BRITAIN IN THE CITY OF OXFORD
AT THE ALDEN PRESS

CONTENTS

5

PREFACE

THE following pages seem to call for an initial word of apology. My excuse for writing on a subject about which I must necessarily be supposed to know nothing is, first of all, that having ventured to give some conferences to St. Joan's Alliance (Oxford) on the vocation of woman, I was urged to put down what I had said in writing; and secondly, that my main concern is not with the facts of married life but with the theology which lies behind them, and I do not know that mistakes about the facts need invalidate the attempt to state the theological principles.

I must emphasize also that what follows will necessarily give a one-sided picture of life precisely because it is concerned with the vocation of woman and not of man. A great many of the things which are here said to apply to women would also apply, though no doubt from a different angle, if one had been concerned with the vocation of men; as it is, I have been concerned to describe what, as it seems to me, women ought to be trying to do — in other words I have attempted to describe the ideal; whereas, in so far as man comes into the picture, he comes in less as he ought to be than as he usually is — not the ideal but the real. It is necessary to stress this fact, lest it appear that one is unfairly discriminating, and putting all the influences for good on one side of the total picture to the exclusion of the other. The man has his equally great and equally essential part to play; but to describe that could not come within the plan of the book.

To say that one is describing the ideal also calls for a word of caution. You need to know the ideal, so as to be quite clear what you are aiming at; but that does not alter the fact that in real life you never attain it, and are often

7

tempted to despair of ever even remotely approaching it.
In this context, moreover, you may be tempted to despair
not only of yourself but of the other, or others, with whom
your life has to be shared: to do your part successfully is
not a thing that depends on you alone. It should, then,
be borne in mind all the way through the following pages
that, if the picture they paint of the ideal is the true one,
the fact that reality seems little likely to approximate to it
in any measurable future is no cause for discouragement:
this Rome, like many others and more than most, will
not be built in a day; and often you may find that while
the surface of things looks black indeed there are hidden
processes, going on beneath the surface, which are full of
promise; and in any case you will find eventually that in
the most important sense to have tried is to have achieved.
You do the best you can, and leave it to God to decide
what the measure of success shall be; you sow, but the
reaping you leave to his wisdom and his love.

G. V.

I

SEEK YE FIRST THE KINGDOM

SEEK ye first, said our Lord, the kingdom of heaven. We are to think, in these meditations, of the vocation of catholic women living in the world and trying to work for Christ in the world; and I want to consider with you some of the great basic facts by which, as it seems to me, any such life must be guided and shaped. In order to do that, I want to set before you the figures of four great catholic women, or rather of three great catholic women and one great symbol of catholic womanhood. And first let us think of St. Catherine of Siena.

We have been told by the Vicar of Christ that this is to be an age of catholic action, an age in which the Church's life is to be especially expressed, and its redeeming work in the world especially fulfilled, by the laypeople; and St. Catherine might well be the patron of woman's share in that lay apostolate. She was a religious, it is true — she is the great glory of the Third Order of St. Dominic — but she lived and worked in the world as any dominican tertiary may do to-day; and she used her immense wisdom and power to do just the sort of work that most needs doing to-day. You have to follow where she led.

She was, I suppose, the greatest woman of her century: she was certainly one of the greatest women Europe has ever seen. She began with no advantages of birth, education, influence; yet we find her overcoming all opposition, acquiring an international renown, advising princes and being called upon to arbitrate between contending states, inducing the Pope, in the teeth of powerful opposition, to return to Rome from Avignon, being herself called to

Rome later on to help in the shaping of papal policy, and playing a part of unique importance when the terrible scandal of the great schism fell upon the Church. Where did her power come from? What had gone before? There are two lessons we must learn from her.

We are told that once when her confessor was preaching in the dominican church, word was brought to him that Catherine was dead. He refused to believe it, finished his sermon, and then went round to her house, where he found her apparently lifeless and surrounded by weeping friends and disciples. Still he refused to believe that she was dead, and took her hand, and presently she did indeed return to consciousness of her surroundings. And then she in her turn could only weep, and repeat over and over again: Oh, I am so unhappy. *Vidi arcana*, she explained later on: I have seen the secret things of God; and she could not bear to come back from them to the world of sin and suffering and blindness. But that is not the end of the story. We are told again that later on when Catherine was one day rapt in ecstasy, and was begging to be taken back to those secret things that she had seen and possessed for a time, our Lord rebuked her — and rebuked her for her *egoism*.

Pope Pius XII, in his encyclical *Mystici Corporis*, applies to the Church the words of St. Paul: The head cannot say to the feet, I have no need of you. Christ, he tells us, *needs* his members, that his redemptive work in the world may be carried out — not because he himself is weak, but because he so willed it for the greater glory of the Church; so that it is in fact certain that the salvation of many depends on the prayers and penances of Christ's faithful and on the part they play in sharing in his work. That is the first lesson we must learn from Catherine's story: that there is such a thing as the danger of a selfish pursuit of holiness. If you are trying hard to live the catholic life, if you are trying daily to find God and live always close to him, if you really want, not in sentiment but in deed and in truth, to put on Christ and be transformed into his likeness, then you have to make sure that you are not forgetting what he said to his apostles: By this shall men know you are my disciples, that you have love one for another. You have to make sure that you are not forgetting the words of St. John in his turn: If any man say, I love God, and hate his brother, he is a liar.

For this is indeed the very stuff of christian holiness. He took upon himself our humanity that he might raise us to his divinity: you are to put on Christ and so, with Christ and in Christ, to come to union with the Godhead; but this is the God who so loved the world that he sent his only-begotten Son to save it; this is the Christ who saved and saves; and in so far as you do come to this union which, even in this life is your destiny you cannot remain absorbed in it and forget the world as long as in the world there are souls to save and work to be done: you must come down again from the mountains of vision, still with Christ and in Christ, and in the power of the vision, and with all the urgency of the love of Christ, you must set yourself to the work he needs you to do.

Wisdom is an end in itself: to try to justify it by its practical effects in terms of power is to degrade it; but at the same time it is perfected, like all experience, when it is expressed and its richness diffused. The christian ideal of wisdom is not a cold, still, impassible contemplation of abstract truth: it is the vision of the Truth who is also Love; and therefore it necessarily impels to loving activity. That is why we read in the praise of wisdom in the Old Testament the assertion, perhaps surprising at first sight, that wisdom is more active than all active things. St. Catherine of Siena wrote a book, the *Dialogue*; and you would have to search far before you found a book

written by man which enshrined a deeper wisdom; but it
was the same Catherine who toiled in the hospitals of
Siena and tended the leper, or who, although in great
pain, went to and fro across Europe to bring peace to
men. To be truly wise is to have learnt to see God; but to
see God is also to see and love and labour for the world he
has made.

But there is a second, and complementary, lesson to be
learnt in this story of Catherine of Siena. Where did she
find the power to do the work she did? (For it is not only
the immensity of her labours that is so astonishing: it is
still more the way in which unlikely people listened to her,
were charmed and changed by her, surrendered to her
and obeyed her.) What is it that you must do in your
turn if you are to be like her? The answer is simple. She
was reproached for her egoism; but she was already a
saint when she was reproached, and her egoism, if you
compare it with our mean and niggling little selfishnesses,
was a white-hot fire of selfless love: she had already given
herself wholly to God. And that is the hard thing; but it is
the essential. The second danger we have to beware of is
the danger of supposing that as long as we love the world
and labour for it, as seems best to us, we have nothing else
to do. This is a greater danger than the first. It is wrong
to seek God in such a way as to forget our duty to the
world; but at least if we do we are not putting secondary
things first. If we think we can help humanity without
first trying to find God, if we try to love humanity without
trying first of all to love God, then we are indeed sub-
ordinating the infinite to the finite, we are in danger of
falling into practical idolatry. And we are in danger also
of defeating our own ends: for we like to think that we are
quite capable of deciding for ourselves how best to help
others, and it is only perhaps when our schemes are
brought to nothing and disaster comes upon us that we

realize that we are fools. And then perhaps God leads us, through our better knowledge of ourselves, to a deeper wisdom; and we begin all over again: begin to learn that if we want to love the world in such a way as to help and not harm it we must first of all listen to God; and that unless we search for him above all other things we miss the deepest reality and the primary purpose of life.

To study the life of Catherine, as indeed of any other saint, is to realize that true wisdom and power are the fruit of a long, hard struggle: the struggle to find God in the silence and solitude of daily prayer; the struggle to be transformed into his likeness by becoming wholly obedient to his will, and so learning the lesson of what is called detachment. As our Lord spent thirty years of hidden preparation for his work, and three years in achieving it, so Catherine in her turn had first her period of solitude and penance, and only then her brilliant spell of work in the world. Certainly we shall misunderstand her entirely if we think of this early period as a dour, thin-lipped, lack-lustre thing: she was as a child so merry that they nicknamed her Joy, she exulted in the splendours of art which surrounded her, and still her feast is celebrated with flowers because she loved them so much; but it remains true that for three years she lived in silence, scarcely left the house except to go to church, and subjected herself to an intense asceticism. It was the necessary training for what was to come; it was also the singleminded carrying out of our Lord's injunction, Seek ye first the kingdom of heaven; it was the achieving of the *unum necessarium*, the one thing necessary.

But what was the perfect fruit of this period of trial and training? It was not the vision of the secret things of God during her mystical death, though that in itself is something beyond our aspiring. It was not in her cry to be dissolved and be again with Christ, though that is

something of which our earth-bound spirits can only
dream from afar. There are four stages in this extraordinary and dramatic life; and to see them in their order
is to have the two lessons we have been considering
combined into one; and it is the third step in the story
which is the climax and the clue to the whole.

It is an incident heavily veiled in mystery. One thing
is beyond dispute: however we interpret the thing itself,
its meaning for our own lives is clear. The period of
intense solitude is over; the secret things have been
revealed; the cry of desire to be united again and for ever
with Christ has been met with the reproach of egoism; our
Lord is teaching her the lesson of divine love for men. And
then one day the lesson, we are to suppose, is learnt in its
fullness. Catherine is in ecstasy; and later she tells her
confessor that Christ has appeared to her and taken away
her heart. The good man's logical mind is outraged: If
you were without a heart, he tells her, you would be dead.
But she insists that she is telling the truth; and so she goes
on for some days; and then our Lord appears to her again,
and gives her back not her own heart but his own. What
does it mean, to have the heart of Christ? It means in the
first place to be filled entirely with the love of God; but it
means also to have within one the love that toiled and
suffered and died in pity and sorrow for the world, and
that will not rest till the redemptive process is fulfilled to
the end. It is to have the love that will never be quenched
by enmity or betrayal, nor disgusted by sin and squalor.
It is to have the heart that can draw all things to itself,
because it has already given them the power to love by
being itself broken on the Cross.

You have had the stage of preparatory training and
searching for God; you have had the stage of complete
absorption in the love of God; now you have this third
stage which is both climax and introduction: climax

14

because here is the completion of the growth in union with God, and the entire identity of will with the will of God, which prayer and detachment have wrought; introduction because the fourth stage inevitably follows as the expression of what has been learnt and suffered and done — the stage of unstinted and redemptive sharing in the suffering of the sin-racked world; and this period too has its climax, the further mysterious experience in which Catherine, having now indeed begged to be allowed to take on herself the sin and pain of the Church, felt her shoulders crushed beneath the weight of the *navicella*, the ship of Peter, and was in fact stricken with a paralysis which ended some days later in her death.

Seek ye first the kingdom, and the rest shall be added unto you. That is the thing we learn from the life of Catherine: that first we must seek for God and be made one with him, and that then we shall turn again to the world, but turn in true love and wisdom and in the power of God, and that only so shall we share as we ought in the redemptive work of Christ. It would of course be wrong to suppose that we must wait until we have reached the identity of will with God which the exchange of hearts symbolizes before we begin to work in the world: if we did that we should achieve little, most of us. But it does mean that we must be clear about the order of importance; it does mean that we must be trying, above all, to be united with God in mind and heart and will, lest all the rest be a service not of the world but of ourselves. It does mean that all the time we must be schooling ourselves to grow, as Catherine did, in prayer and detachment.

Let us think first of all about the life of prayer. What does it mean? It means three things. You may not be called to retire into solitude for a long period as Catherine was; that is not the essential. There are plenty of men and women who have learnt to be saints in the midst of a busy life. The essential thing is to have some space of time, half an hour if possible but at the very least a quarter, set apart every day for the purpose of prayer in silence and solitude; and to remain faithful to that. You can find God in the midst of a busy life; but not if you never for a moment withdraw your mind from its business and wait upon him. Those who are filled with zeal for activity for the world, but are tempted to dismiss the need of daily prayer as a luxury in such times of crisis as these, may learn a lesson from the story of Elias. You remember how he too, a man of tremendously powerful personality, and filled with zeal to triumph over God's enemies — but to triumph by a harsh display of might and wrath and violence — he had indeed triumphed, he had brought down fire from heaven upon the idolaters and consumed them and was jubilant, thinking he had served God well; and then he saw his triumph turn to ashes, and was forced to flee for his life. And then, in his humiliation and self-contempt, he threw himself down under a juniper tree and begged God that he might die, because he was no better than his fathers. And God vouchsafed him a vision, and showed him why his success had turned to failure; for first there came a great wind, which overthrew the mountains and broke the rocks in pieces, but the Lord was not in the wind; and then there came an earthquake, but the Lord was not in the earthquake; and then there came a fire, but still the Lord was not there. But after all these symbols of wrath and might and terror there came the whisper of a gentle wind, or, as another version has it, the sound of a still, small voice; and when the prophet heard it he covered his head with his mantle for he knew that this was the Lord. It was to teach him first of all that you cannot fight for a merciful, gentle God except with the weapons of a merciful, gentle God; but perhaps we may see in it too a further symbolism. For this zeal without

wisdom, this determination to fight for God without understanding the nature of God, this is the very thing we shall
do unless we set out to seek him before we attempt to
serve him; and if we seek him we must seek not in sound
and fury but in the deep silence in which alone his voice
can be heard. But the ability to hear, the ability to open
the mind to God, is something that can only be won by
constant and regular effort. That is why you must have
every day[1] your time set apart for prayer; and why
you must refuse to be discouraged by an apparent lack
of progress or by dryness, however persistent, and lack of
devout emotions: the only practical test of the value of
your prayer is whether it makes you more eager to do God's
will. You have to find the type of prayer best suited to you
individually: some are best served at the beginning by a
form of meditation, whether elaborate or simple, as a
prelude and incentive to acts of adoration, sorrow, trust,
love and so on; others by simple aspirations which are
themselves prayer and can be repeated over and over
again, and mould the soul to their pattern. You have to
expect distractions and refuse to be dismayed or depressed
by them: all that is required is that you go on, day by day,
till God in his own time, if he wills it, calls you to other and
higher forms of prayer and of union with him.

The second element in the life of prayer is the Church's
liturgy. That is a thing in which we can all share, and
must share. We may have neither time nor opportunity
to take part in the full liturgical cycle as you find it

---

[1] You have to be prepared to give up even prayer, on occasion, at the
call of charity; and sometimes there will be days when the half-hour really
is impossible. That is not necessarily a cause for worry unless such days
begin to be frequent or to turn into a whole succession of days; what is
important is that the habit remain a habit, and even on the busiest days a
few minutes' recollection is always possible. Moreover, a fixed daily time
for prayer is a useful help to forming the habit, but it need not be too
rigid; and if we find it invaded by other calls upon us we can usually, with
a little forethought, find another time that will do as well.

carried out in a benedictine monastery; but we can all assist at Mass. No need to emphasize the primary importance of daily Mass: it is the substance, the foundation on which all the rest, the life of prayer and detachment, must be built; but we sometimes forget the importance also of the liturgy as such. To take part in the Mass, to say the words of the Mass with the priest and perform the appropriate gestures and movements, is to let the Church teach us to pray. It teaches us first of all to pray with body and mind alike: to make our entire personality an offering of worship. It lifts our prayer into a higher level and intensity of being, by embodying it in the total prayer of the Church and its Head. And because it can mould us gradually, by its deep and varied appeal to senses and feeling, mind and heart, into conformity with the attitude of adoring self-offering which its symbolism expresses, it can lead us to the life of prayer in the fullest sense: not only making it more easy to find in our times of mental prayer a real communion with God, but also turning our whole lives with all that they contain into a continuous act of worship and offering, and so transforming us gradually into beings of praise, which is indeed our destiny.

This leads us to consider the third element in the life of prayer, which is precisely the habitual sense of the presence of God. Here again you have to be prepared for a long and arduous struggle; and indeed without the liturgy and the daily time of prayer it would be an impossibility. It does not mean, of course, that you have to be all the time consciously thinking of God: you have your work to do, you have to concentrate on other things. It does mean that you have to acquire the habit of constantly turning back to God, to the realization of his presence, both as present everywhere by his immensity and as dwelling within the soul as object of love and knowledge through the supernatural gift of grace. The first step is to learn to make use of odd moments of leisure to think of God, be conscious of him, and speak to him; and again, without trying to do violence to the mind by a rigid control, to spend some of the freedom which manual work affords in a simple form of prayer. Similarly you have to remind yourself, from time to time, that the materials of your work and play and all your daily life are hallowed by the presence of infinity within them and about them: and while, where beautiful things are concerned, you remember that it is the love of God that makes them lovely, you have to remember also that he and his love are present also in the weak and the mean and the ugly. But always, lest you fall into a woolly and sentimental sort of pantheism, you have to remember that the God who is thus present in the things he has made is the same God whom in your prayers you are learning to know and to worship, the Infinite Transcendent. And then, we are told, if you go on faithfully making these acts of adoring awareness of God's presence, they will become habitual to you, and the sense of this presence will become natural to you; so that in the end, even when you are concentrating on other matters, it will never be wholly lost to you.[1]

And then you will be at least beginning to have within you the heart of Christ; for you cannot live habitually in his presence without habitually judging and willing in his presence: thoughts and desires will tend more and more to be referred to him and determined by him, until in the end you have that fullness of life which is wisdom in the mind and holiness in the will, mind and will made wholly one with the True and the Good, and therefore able, like Catherine, to love the whole world and work for it even unto death.

The ideal of living always in God's presence can provide

[1] Cf. that charming and valuable little treatise: *The Practice of the Presence of God*, by Brother Lawrence.

19

us with a clue to the next point we have to consider, the christian doctrine of what is called detachment; for if we live always in God's sight and try to act always according to his will, our attitude towards created things will necessarily come to be modelled on his. The name detachment is indeed an unfortunate one: it sounds negative and niggardly, and can give rise to serious misunderstanding. Perhaps we should do well to speak rather of poverty of spirit, or indeed quite simply of the right love of creatures. For detachment is not a denial of life but a denial of death; not a disintegration but the condition of wholeness; not a refusal to love but the determination to love truly, deeply and fully.

Let us state the thing first in terms of the apparent contradiction with which the gospel presents us. We have already been thinking of the words of our Lord, By this shall men know that you are my disciples, that you have love one for another; and when he gives his followers the two great commandments of love, of God and of men, he tells them that the second is like unto the first. Yet it was he too who said at another time: If any man come to me and hate not his father and mother and sister and brother, he cannot be my disciple. Can these opposing statements be reconciled?

There would be no opposing statements were it not for the fact of sin, which gives an ambiguity to the way we use the word love. Too often we say love when we mean merely self-love: we say we love this or that but we mean simply that we like the pleasure they can give us; with their own well-being we are not concerned. And to treat thus the things that God has made, our fellow creatures, is to offend him; for the love with which he made them makes them lovable in themselves.

But more than that, to treat things simply as means to our own pleasure is to assume over them a dominion which is not ours; to try, in the last resort, to be as gods, and so to refuse to obey God's will rather than our own. Real love, on the other hand, is expressed in the words of the old definition, to will another's good: which implies that we allow no hardship or sacrifice to deter us from helping those we love, we look always to what is best for *them*, we love them therefore not as mere means to our pleasure but as ends in themselves, as beings whom it is a joy and a privilege to serve. But to love them for themselves, for what they really are, is to love them as God's creatures, whose first duty is to him; and therefore while selfish covetousness turns creatures into God's rivals because it tries to arrogate to itself their creaturely relationship to God, real love is based upon that relationship: it wills the good of the one loved, but it knows that that good is to be found in loving obedience to the will of God.

The love which is really only pride and covetousness, then, is incompatible with the love of God; real love on the contrary is a part of the love of God. And so, if we think of pride and covetousness as love, then before we can be Christ's disciples we must reverse our whole attitude: we must hate; if, on the other hand, we understand love aright, then indeed we are to rest assured that it will be through that love that we shall be known as his disciples.

We must speak then of a false love and a true: and whereas true love is not only permitted but commanded, false love is the stuff of all sin, for it is egoism, and egoism is rooted in pride, and pride is the primal sin. You are saying in effect that anything which attracts you is your creature; you can do what you like with it; the power of decision, to do this or that, rests with you; in other words you are committing the sin of self-idolatry, you are denying the absolutes of truth and goodness, you are making yourself your own god. The thing can be seen at its

21

crudest in those sins of rapacious greed for pleasure in which human beings treat one another as toys; we are less ready to realize that the same is true, substantially, of those sins in which there is true love of another human being but in which none the less we flout the will of God, we make ourselves the arbiters of good and evil: in these, too, there is the same essential sin, for it is still the human judgment which is deified, the divine which is denied. Sometimes indeed this problem will present itself in terms of an unbearable tension between the claims of a true human love and obedience to God: all one's instincts and feelings, all one's judgment and deep desire for another's good will rise up and cry out, I cannot do this, I cannot cause all this suffering and all this harm for the sake of a principle; and then you have to try to remember that in fact we just do not know with any certainty what, on a long view, is for another's good; we just cannot foresee the consequences of our actions, we just do not understand the depths of the problem of suffering, and the only thing we can do, if we want to be wise, is to trust in the judgments of God. You remember the words of Job: Even though he slay me, yet will I trust him. There may be times when you will have to say, Even though he slay my friend, my lover, my country, yet will I trust him — and continue to obey him.

But the false love is not only expressed in a self-willed choice of evil in defiance of the law of God: detachment means much more than the avoidance of that. There is a second sort of choice, not of evil as against good, but of a thing good in itself as against what is God's will for you at any given moment. You may say there is nothing wrong in this action, this interest, this possession, in itself, and you may be right; but it may not be God's will for you, it may not be part of your particular vocation; and then, if you insist on clinging to it, you are still committing the primal sin of pride and egoism, you are still making your-self the arbiter of what is right for you. Here we are nearer the core of the doctrine of detachment; for when-ever you say of anything, no matter what it may be, I cannot do without that, I will not do without that, I am going to decide what I do with it or for it or because of it, you are clinging to something in defiance of God, and consequently, however unselfish, however noble, however pure your love of it may be, humanly speaking, it is still to that extent a false love, it is still keeping you from the total service of God.

And supposing you have at long last schooled yourself to put God's will first in everything, to let him decide what you shall have and not have, do and not do: does it follow that you have ceased to love the world of men and of things? On the contrary, it may well mean exactly the opposite: it may well mean that at long last you have really started to love them — to love *them* and not yourself. Perhaps you only now begin to realize that since you are not their master they for their part are not just means but ends, they are to be loved in themselves. You will also find that *all* the things that God has made and that he loves are lovable, and not just those things which you would otherwise have found superficially attractive. But above all, you will love not less but infinitely more than before because, when you have reached this degree of identity with the will of God, you will have been given the heart of Christ as Catherine was; and so you will love with a breadth and depth which no merely human love can compass: you will find that there is nothing so small or so mean as to escape your love, and nothing for which you would not gladly bear, as Christ did, a redeeming cross.

Once realize then that detachment means simply the destruction of the false love in order to give birth to the true, and the danger of misunderstanding it disappears.

So also does the apparent contradiction in the words of our Lord. Long ago St. Thomas Aquinas put the matter very simply and very clearly, by quoting the injunction to hate father and mother and adding that this means in so far as they turn us from God: in so far as the love is a false love and not a true. But to understand the thing in theory is not the same, alas, as carrying it out in practice. (There is no holiness without tears.) You have to kill in yourself the love that is wholly selfish, that uses things as mere means, for what you can get out of them; and that is hard enough, but it is only the beginning. You have to kill in yourself the pride which spoils a love that, as far as its created object is concerned, is true and generous enough, but that will not acknowledge the dominion of God; and that is harder. You have to learn to acknowledge that dominion, not only when it is a choice between good and evil, not only when it is a choice between what is good in itself and what is God's will for you here and now, but also in the sense of being prepared and ready in heart to acknowledge and welcome it universally and without qualification in the future, no matter what calls it may make upon your generosity, no matter what crosses it may invite you to bear; and that is the hardest of all.

The English mystic Walter Hilton, in his *Scale of Perfection*, has some valuable passages which reveal the difficulty of this poverty and freedom of spirit even when outwardly the world has been wholly renounced. He is writing to an anchoress: she has forsaken riches and possessions and is shut in a dungeon, but has she forsaken covetousness? It is easier, he says, to forsake worldly possessions than to forsake the love of them. Perhaps her covetousness remains with her but is changed from great things to small — it is a shrewd hit at the danger which besets those who embrace a life of voluntary poverty, the danger of clinging to little valueless things with all the tenacity of a miser clutching his hoard. But in any case, even if you were reduced to owning absolutely nothing, still you could fail to have detachment and freedom of spirit; for still you could hanker after the things you lacked, you could want them as your own, apart from God, and the lack of them could be more of a hindrance to the perfect love and service of God than ever the possession would have been.

These things are best seen in an example. There is someone you love very much: does detachment bid you to cease loving him? No, of course not; but it bids you be sure that the love is true and not false, really love and not just covetousness. It bids you learn to see the love as God's gift, not as your own property; as part of your vocation and not as an escape from it. More than that, it bids you leave your possession and enjoyment of it wholly in his hands: supposing you want to see the person you love, and there is no reason why you should not, but God intervenes and prevents you: then you must not rebel, you must not try to circumvent his will, but more than that you must not grumble, you must not think yourself ill-treated, you must not brood upon your injuries — the thing is not yours, anyway, but his, and you have to try to be ready to say, not of each particular incident as it arises but of your love as a whole, Even though he take it wholly from me, yet will I trust him.

Our purpose in these meditations is to think of the vocation of woman in the world. But here you have the essential condition of all work, and of every vocation, in the world. You cannot work for God in the world unless you love the world; but you cannot love the world truly unless you have learnt or at least are learning day by day to love God above all and all things in God, unless you have learnt to live the life of prayer and of poverty of spirit. Seek ye first the kingdom of heaven: it does not

mean that you must seek only your own sanctification and
forsake your responsibilities to the world; it does not mean
that you must reduce your love of created things to a thin
colourless simulacrum of detached benevolence as the
words are nowadays understood; it means exactly the
contrary. The more you love God the more you will love
the world, because the more you will share in his love of
it. The more you can kill in yourself the false love which
values things only for what you can get out of them, the
more you will see them and love them as they really are.
The more you rid yourself of possessiveness and pride, and
free yourself of the slavery that ties you down to your
possessions and the haunting dread of losing them, the
greater your love will grow both in breadth and in intensity until in the end it embraces, like the love of God, the
whole of the sin-laden and suffering world. Seek first the
kingdom of heaven, and all the rest shall be added unto
you.

When we think, then, of Catherine of Siena as of a
leader and guide in whose footsteps we are to follow, let
us salute in her first of all her *prayer*: the one thing necessary, the substance of life, from which action, if it is to
be Christ-like and redeeming, must, and will inevitably,
flow. Let us salute in her, secondly, her *wisdom*: it was a
wisdom that she learnt in prayer — not the acquired
wisdom of a powerful intellect but the infused wisdom of a
humble heart, the intuitive grasp of truth, the love-
knowledge, which as we shall see later is the wisdom most
proper to woman's vocation in the world. Let us salute
in her, finally, the third condition without which no
Christ-like action is possible: her poverty and freedom of
spirit, her *detachment*. We are told that after her mysterious
exchange of hearts with Christ she always prayed, not,
Lord, I offer thee my heart, but, Lord, I offer thee thy
heart; we have to remind ourselves that out of the long

and laborious struggle with its three stages, the struggle to choose God's will instead of evil, to choose God's will instead of what is good in itself but not his will for us, to choose God's will universally and without reservation, no matter what the future may bring, in an act of total self-offering — out of this struggle there comes the glory of possessing the heart of Christ, with all its immensity of divine and universal love, and all its immensity of power to heal and help the suffering world.[1] If we try, slowly and painfully but doggedly, to follow in Catherine's footsteps and seek first as she did the kingdom of heaven, then we need have no fear that our efforts to serve the world will be frustrated or end in failure: for we shall more and more fully express in our lives his will and his redeeming love, we shall share in the desire of his heart and in his power to fulfil it; and we shall not worry about the results of our work, the success or failure that the future may bring, because we shall be more and more content to do what he tells us, and in the end the rest will be added unto us.

---

[1] Detachment explains also the two ways in which the Bible speaks of the world. St. John tells us, Love not the world: he means the abode of Mammon, the spirit of worldliness which rejects God and makes its own god of money or power or pleasure. That is egoism, the false love. But he also tells us, God so loved the world as to give his Son, to save it: and that world is the earth and its fullness, his handiwork, and especially the race of men his children; and to love that world as such is part of man's love of God, the true love.

II

THE MYSTICAL BODY AND THE VOCATION OF MOTHERHOOD

His mother kept all these words in her heart. (Luke ii. 51)

THE head cannot say to the feet, I have no need of you: Christ needs the members of his mystical Body to carry out his redemptive work in the world; that we have already considered. But you remember how Pope Pius XII, in his encyclical *Mystici Corporis*, is at pains to stress the fact already pointed out by St. Paul, that different members have by definition different functions to fulfil according to their different gifts; and if you hold that grace perfects nature, takes what we are by nature and makes that the material of the supernaturalized life, then you must hold also that the differences of natural as well as supernatural gifts determine the function the christian is to fulfil in the Church. That is indeed the basis of the christian doctrine of vocation.

Now underneath all the varieties of individual qualities and characteristics there lies the greatest of all natural differentiations: which is that between man and woman. It is true that we are none of us wholly male or female in our make-up; but it remains permissible to speak of the male mind or the female mind, and therefore of the vocation of man and the vocation of woman, inasmuch as there are some qualities of mind and soul which ought to be predominant in man and others which ought to be predominant in woman. Let me add that very great people, the genius and the saint, seem to stand above these differentiations and to unite in themselves, in creative harmony, the qualities of both sexes; and we all have to try to be saints, so that for all of us the ideas we have to consider are bound to be ultimately relevant.

His mother kept all these words in her heart. This text gives us a clue to the essence of the matter. If you look at primitive societies, where human nature is at its simplest, you find a clear-cut division: the man is the bread-winner, the active one, the builder; the woman is the housewife, the receptive one, the conserver. It is the man who goes out to hunt; the woman who stays behind to preserve the home and the family. And as the intellectual life of a community evolves, the same fundamental distinction persists: it is the man, the builder and legislator, who represents reason; the woman, the conserver and consoler, who represents intuition. The man adventures in ideas, in science and philosophy, and builds up what is new; the woman conserves the deep lasting unchanging wisdom in her heart.

You hear a great deal nowadays about the equality of the sexes: there is a great danger here. If you are trying to defend woman from the degradation of being treated as a chattel, from the horrors of child-marriage and so on, then of course you are wholly right: these things are a crime against human nature and against the laws of God. But be careful: if by equality you mean an obliteration of the difference between the sexes you will end by destroying the integrity of both. For the whole idea and purpose of the difference is that the two together are complementary: they complete one another precisely because they differ from one another. Man and woman are meant to have the equality of true companionship; but true companionship does not exclude a subordination on one plane. If we had begun this meditation with some of the sayings of St. Paul about woman, would you have been irritated or depressed? If so, you would have been wrong. You will

not achieve the freedom and dignity of woman by trying
to turn her into a man; you will only destroy her, and
man as well.

On one level there is a subordination, there is obedience.
But be comforted: on another level it is woman who
indisputably reigns. Her special role, spiritually, intel-
lectually, as well as biologically and economically, is just
as necessary to man as his is to her. They are partners,
fellow-workers — you ruin everything if you try to give
them both the same work.

St. Paul tells us that it is only when Christ dwells in
the heart that we may hope to comprehend with all the
saints the length and breadth and height and depth, so as
to be filled with all the fullness of God. It is the destiny of
every christian, since every christian is called to become a
saint; but it has a special relevance to the vocation of
woman, for it is this sense of length and breadth and
height and depth that she in particular is meant, because
of her natural gifts first of all, to bring to the human
family. Man, the rational, active builder, tends to be
concerned with the immediate and apparent needs of life,
with the surface, and in consequence to take the short
view; woman is meant by nature to be slower to leap to
conclusions: it is for her to keep in her heart the words, the
experiences, which life brings to them both; and having
kept them in her heart to come to understand them in a
different way. She must know the length: she must be
able to take, not so much rationally as intuitively, a long
view; she must see beyond the immediate necessities and
advantages, and sense ultimate effects. She must know
the breadth: it is easy for the man, all too easy, in the
struggle for life, to find himself involved in facile enmities;
it is for her to preserve in herself and in him the sense of
the unity of the human family and indeed of all the
creatures of God. She must know the height: it is easy

for the man to become so wrapped up in his human work and human striving for progress that he comes to measure all things by purely human standards, or at least forgets that there are things that matter even more than daily bread; she must preserve his human labours along the horizontal line of human progress from the dangers of shallowness and perhaps idolatry by her upward, vertical striving of spirit towards divinity — she must be always bringing back a humanist world to the sense of God. She must know the depth. It is her heaviest cross and her greatest glory. The humanist world is a shallow world, a world of false and facile optimism, inasmuch as it forgets the fact of sin, or tries to ignore it. But you cannot ignore the underworld of life with impunity. Either you must go down into it, suffer it, understand it, and over-come it; or you can try to forget it for a time, and then, sooner or later, it will rise up against you and destroy you. And when a whole civilization tries thus to forget the sense of depth it may live very placidly on the surface for a while; it may make immense progress, but still on the surface; and then its nemesis too will come upon it, and it will find itself driven back to the darkness of the caves. That is why, even on a purely natural reckoning, we so desperately need the vocation of woman in the world of to-day; and why we need so desperately this aspect of the fullness of life of the saints.

Let us think here, then, of the woman who most perfectly and most completely fulfilled the vocation of woman: the mother of God. We may remind ourselves first of all, in view of what we were thinking about before, that she was fit to be the mother because she was fit to be the bride, and she was fit to be the bride because she makes her *fiat* absolute and unconditional: Behold the handmaid of the Lord, be it done to me according to thy word. That identity of will with the will of God, which we were thinking of before as the condition of all Christ-like action in the world, is here the condition of the coming of Christ himself into the world. Eve, the mother of mankind, had brought evil into the world through self-will, through setting her own will in opposition to the will of God; Mary, the mother of redeemed mankind, brought the Saviour into the world by reversing the primal sin, by identifying her will utterly with the will of God, by fulfilling once again in its entirety the essential destiny of the human soul — to be the handmaid of the Lord.

But in what sense is she the mother of mankind, the universal mother? First of all because she gives birth to the new race, the new world, through her Son in whom the world is renewed. Secondly because a mother is always involved in the work and destiny of her son; and the work of Mary's Son is the redemption of the race of men. Thirdly because her acceptance of her destiny is at the same time an acceptance, on behalf of humanity, of the spiritual marriage between humanity and divinity, brought about first of all in the person of Christ and thence, through and in him, though in a different sense, in all who believe in his name and do his will.

She is the universal mother; and that very fact is in itself one of the reasons why she is the supreme type of womanhood. There is an element of motherhood in every love that is true and deep; and it is this that is at the very centre of the vocation of woman. Having learnt with Mary to say with her, *ecce ancilla*, behold the hand-maid of the Lord, you must then go on to imitate her in this above all if your proper vocation in the world is to be fulfilled.

The rational mind of the male tends to take the short view, to become involved in rivalries and enmities, to ignore the heights of the eternal hills and the depths of evil and misery; and for any or all of these reasons the

rational schemes of the male and all his work of building
and all his ambitions tend to come tumbling down, sooner
or later, in ruins about him; and it is then that woman is
meant to find her vocation as mother of man, and her
share in the universal motherhood of Mary. Sometimes
indeed it is only this catastrophe which can enable her to
recall man to the sense of length and breadth and height
and depth: when all goes well he refuses to listen, he meets
her wisdom with a parade of logic and beats it down; and
it is not till he has seen his own world crashing about him,
seen the chaos to which he has brought himself, that he
comes back to be re-born in the womb of her pity and
realizes belatedly that she was right, realizes perhaps that
all the time he knew unconsciously that she was right and
that his parade of reason was only an escapist mechanism
of rationalization. But she for her part will throw away
her destiny if in the moments of failure and abjection she
despises him; if she does that she fails herself. She has to
preserve her faith in him; and she has to preserve his own
faith in himself, in his ability to start again, to re-build in a
new spirit what is broken or to build something new and
more worth while.

, Here she may have to meet her greatest temptation, in
this moment when her essential vocation is fulfilled. It is
the temptation to make herself the triumphant rival of the
work the man is meant to do. Not that the temptation is
confined to these moments; on the contrary; but it is here
that it can be most acute.

Think of the normal evolution of the married life of a
man and a woman. They marry because they love each
other; but they marry in order that together they may
build something other than themselves, build the family.
In other words, the man is not only to be husband but
father and breadwinner as well; the woman is not only
to be wife but mother and housewife. Their glory is to

share together as ministers of God's omnipotence in the making of new immortal beings, and to help them to grow up in God's likeness and lead them back safely to God. But they have to learn not only that that is God's will for them, but also, sometimes, that that is the perfect fulfilment of their love; and sometimes the lesson is a hard one; sometimes they can be tempted to resent their destiny as a distraction from their love, to go on for ever being lovers and escaping the responsibilities of being makers. If they do that they will never have the fullness of life or the fullness of love; they will never grow up.

The temptation for the woman is twofold. The man has his home and his career; he may neglect one of them for the sake of the other; she for her part may be tempted to view the career either as a rival, withdrawing him from her, or at least as a part of his life in which she has no share. In either case she fails to fulfil her destiny. For it is no longer his career, his work; it is their career, their work. She is dependent on him, on the results of the work, that the home may be preserved; but he for his part is dependent on her, on the wisdom she can bring him if she has learnt her destiny aright, on her faith in him, on her love and the strength it gives her to support them and give them hope in times of crisis and distress. She has to learn her particular wisdom, she has to learn her particular work — the domestic arts — she has to learn the particular qualities she needs as a wife, precisely in order to help him achieve his vocation and to share in his work. Every christian has to think of the work God has given him to do as being more important than his own wellbeing; she has to think this of the work God has given her *in him*. But it may happen that he for his part becomes so absorbed in his career that he loses interest in her; and it may be only failure that will bring him back; and it is then, when that happens, that she has to meet the keenest temptation, the temptation to spend all her energies simply on retaining his love permanently instead of giving him new heart for the work. She must, of course, want to retain his love; but she must try to re-integrate his life, not destroy a part of it: her vocation is still to minister to the work — and if she does that, it is surely probable that her faith and love and strength will themselves win back for her the fullness of his love, whereas if she sets herself up as a rival she will at best only triumph for a time, for you cannot frustrate half of a man's nature indefinitely.

That is her first temptation. The second comes of the duality of her life as wife and mother. When she is first married, perhaps the man's predominant attitude will be one of adoration; she will be in a position to command. The power that sex gives you over another's will is a terrible thing: it can be used to teach and to save, but it can also be used to destroy and ruin. Her temptation will be to preserve that relationship unchanged; to preserve at all costs the power, and therefore the endowments which give the power. And again if she does that she will be throwing away not only his destiny but her own. Her part, in the last resort, is not to command and make decisions but to cause him to command and make decisions; otherwise he will never reach his full stature as a man. But she herself will never reach her full stature as a woman unless she goes on to fulfil her destiny as a mother. Her life of labour in kitchen and nursery, with all the demands it puts upon her of courage and patience and dogged endurance: it is this that can teach her, more than anything, her own deep wisdom. But only if she does it wholeheartedly. You cannot create a family, a home, unless you love your children completely; but you cannot love them completely unless, feeling their dependence on you, you give yourself entirely to them. That is why a woman has to stop being a goddess on a pedestal

and become a worker in a kitchen and a nursery. And a
year or two goes by, and one day the man realizes that
his companion is not a goddess but a hard-worked woman,
beginning to show signs of the work and worry she has had
to contend with; and then — and it is part of *his* growth to
fullness — he should be moved with compassion to think
that it is her devotion to him and to his children that has
brought about this change; and he should be filled with a
sense of the family's dependence on him, and a determination to take care of it and provide for it and cherish
it, cost what it may. And if they both accept their vocation in this way, in the fullness of the demands it makes on
them, then they learn a deeper love and unity than ever
they could achieve in the more lyrical and idyllic stage of
their career: they fulfil in their lives the image of the Holy
Family.

Mary kept all these words in her heart. It is Joseph who
has to make the decisions; Joseph to whom the angel
speaks when they are to escape into Egypt. It is Joseph
who provides and protects and compassionates. But you
cannot imagine the life at Nazareth without imagining
the wisdom, the perhaps often unspoken wisdom, he
learnt from her; the protective love and pity with which
she too, in her different way, surrounded him; her
identification of herself with the work he had to do. But
above all you cannot imagine the life at Nazareth apart
from the complete self-dedication of Joseph and Mary
alike to the work, the vocation, of their Son. He advanced
in wisdom and age and grace with God and men, St.
Luke tells us: it was under their tutelage, for we are told
also that he went down with them and came to Nazareth
and was subject to them. And when it was time for his
public work, his mother, who had prepared him for it,
so far from detaining him seems to efface herself, to
disappear from the picture — but her heart is in him and

in his work, and if she disappears it is only to reappear when perhaps he may need her, to be there at the end, in her faith and love and courage, to share his cry of dereliction, and to hear him say, It is perfected.

Mary, the Queen of the Seven Swords, knew as no other woman has known the length and breadth and height and depth. It is not only married women, it is all women, who have to share in their degree her vocation of the motherhood of man, and to share it by sharing her wisdom.

She knew the length, she who was told, so early on: Thy own soul a sword shall pierce; seeing in the Child's play the future Passion, seeing — sensing in her heart — in the Passion the glory of the Redemption. She knew the length because she knew, she saw in her Son's story, that immediate failure is often ultimate success and apparent success is often ultimately failure: she knew that what is wisdom to men is often folly to God. And those who share in her vocation have to share in her length of view: theirs is the majesty of bringing up souls for God, their eyes fixed not on the immediate and often illusory objectives of money and social advancement but on the ultimate objective of the fullness of eternal life. And their work is like the work of the Precursor, John the Baptist, who sent his disciples away from him to follow their true destiny when the Master came: they have to wean their children, spiritually as well as physically, teach them to be independent, give them to the world; and though they remain with them, to support them in the background as Mary remained to the end at the foot of the cross, it must be only to help them the better to do the work they have to do. And this is a role which belongs to all who share the vocation of woman, not only to wives and to mothers of families. It belongs to all those who work for the world, even quite apart from the personal relationships that this may involve: there is always the need of bringing the wisdom of the long view to any enterprise, lest it start in a glitter of easy optimism but rapidly end in failure and despair. It belongs in particular to the women of prayer in the Church: for it is their prayer-life which supports the Church's activity and those responsible for it; it is they who stand behind the missionary enterprises, for example, and give them the power to continue undismayed; it is they who stand behind all the activity which attempts to incarnate the truth of God in the material of earthly life, to preserve it from becoming immersed in immediate issues and to give it a sense of its final end.

Mary, the Mother of men, knew the breadth, precisely because of the universality of her love and her motherhood, precisely because she loves all that her Son loves. And the role of women in the world, countering the tendency of men to be immersed in their immediate partisanships and to forget the unity of the human family, makes it especially urgent for them to have within them the heart of Christ and its universality, and in particular to have a sense of the unity of the Mystical Body. In these days above all, when the world is torn by conflict and by hatred, and to hope for the unity of the world seems no more than an idle dream, we need this aspect of woman's gift to the world. We know the words of our Lord: You have heard that it hath been said: Thou shalt love thy neighbour and hate thy enemy; but I say to you: Love your enemies, do good to them that hate you . . . that you may be the children of your Father who is in heaven. We know the words, but we fail to fulfil them. But woman has, even biologically, a relationship to the race as a whole quite different from that of man; its story is recapitulated in her womb and she knows it in the helplessness of infancy, she knows it in the crudities of the fundamental needs and desires in which all men are one; and that gives her a special knowledge and a special responsibility; and she has to learn to see not only the humanity in every human being but the divinity, the presence of God which is in them all and the divine destiny in which they all share. So she must join with Mary in throwing the mantle of her care over all the human family; and then she will join with Mary also in bringing that family back to God.

Mary, the Tower of Ivory, knew the height. You find her first with her hands and eyes uplifted to the message of God made known to her by the angel. You find on her lips the greatest and loveliest of all boasts — behold from henceforth all generations shall call me blessed — but because she is simply and humbly stating a fact, the fact of a glory which comes from God and which she trembles to receive, her eyes are again fixed not on herself but on him that is mighty and hath done great things to her. And you find her again at the end, standing by the Cross, and again her eyes are uplifted to the figure upon it; for you do not read that she, the Tower of Ivory, was weeping; even the horror of the final sword does not cause her to flinch from her faith and her courage, nor to forget that what is folly and failure to men is wisdom and redemption in the eyes of God. She knew the height; she who when she cuddled her child knew that it was also her God, so that her life of devotion to the work of her Son was at the same time, in itself, a life of devotion to her Lord. She knew the height, she whose every action was a preparation for, or a sharing in, the work of redemption, and whose knowledge of the ways and purposes of God was so far removed from the worldly-mindedness of those who thought to find in the Messiah a re-builder of their lost political independence. Those who share her vocation have here again a special duty to-day, when so much sincere desire to improve the lot of humanity is vitiated by its inability to measure what is for the good of man by

reference to eternal truth. The humanist world is roofed
in low by its self-imposed limitations, and stifles men who
perhaps without knowing it long for a sight of the infinite
skies; and its programmes of social reform are apt to end
in arrogance because it lacks the dimension of worship,
and to end in a progressive mechanizing and regimenting
of human nature itself because it fails to realize that the
endless upward striving of humanity is not in the last
resort towards material ends however beneficent, but
towards the supernatural destiny of the sons of God.

Finally, it is as refuge of sinners and comforter of the
afflicted that we salute the mother of God; for she
beyond all other women knew the dimension of depth. If
a woman insists on trying to make her life with a man a
perpetual honeymoon and nothing more, she will never
know the ultimate greatness and the ultimate depths of
love and oneness with which her motherhood might have
adorned her; if you think of our Lady only as the maiden
who is makeless or as the queen of heaven you will only
know a part of her, you will miss the sublimity, you will
also miss the pathos and the nearness, of the mother of
sorrows. It is because she suffered in such closeness to her
Son that she has more than any other woman an understanding of the sins and the sorrows of the world, and a
greater share than any other woman in the wisdom and
the pity of Christ. If you want to know the depths you
have to study the problem of pain and of evil, but to
study it not with the brain merely but with the heart.
The length must give you a sense of the immeasurable
chain of evils that sin begets; the breadth must show you
the immensity of the world's sin and give you a sense of
your share in it, a feeling of responsibility for it because it
weighs down on the shoulders of the members of your
family; the height must reveal to you the density of its
darkness against the flawless purity of the white-hot fire of

God's love; but all this will flare up into life within you only when you yourself have learnt to suffer in your own heart the sorrows of others, and to feel in your own heart the reality of sin.

We were thinking of the way in which a woman can find her destiny at the very moment when man has failed. But without the sense of depth she will miss it because she will despise him for his failure and then everything will be lost. Mary kept all these words in her heart: she had to gain her understanding of the depths through her deep penetration of the mind and heart of God. With us the case is different: there are things we can see all too clearly in ourselves. She had to learn of the sin of man and the mercy of God when she saw and suffered what they did to her Son, and heard his prayer to the Father to forgive them; we are ourselves among them. But our experimental knowledge of evil is worse than useless to us unless we acquire, or rather can become worthy to be given, the ability to see it as she did through the eyes of God. St. Teresa tells us that as a soul progresses towards God there comes a time when the sense of its own sin, as set against the majesty and purity and love of God, becomes an unbearable burden: it is just that awareness, the fruit of many prayers and many trials, that we need above all in the world to-day. It is out of the womb of divine pity, of the love that emptied itself of infinity to take on the form of a man, that redemption is born; and it is in so far as woman can share in that love and that pity that she too can fulfil her essential work.

There can be no peace in the world and therefore no renewal except by the restoration of its unity. But its unity will never be restored by the violent and external regimentations of collectivism; it can only be restored by a recovery on the part of individual human beings of a personal consciousness of unity. There is the unself-

conscious unity of a primitive tribe: we can neither revert
to that nor desire to revert to it. There is the disintegration of an individualist civilization: and that has brought
us to our present pass. There is no way out for us except
the effort to establish consciously a conscious unity, a
conscious family life; which is the same as saying that
peace is the fruit of charity. And here too you have a clear
expression of the vocation of woman. If you think of the
great women who have altered, or laboured to alter, the
face of our civilization — of Elizabeth Fry, of Florence
Nightingale, of Nurse Cavell; of a Catherine of Siena or a
Teresa of Avila — always you seem to find that they are
fighting for the inner values, the deeper values, which
alone make the fulfilments of male ambition bearable.
Patriotism is not enough; justice is not enough; scientific
power is only a servant: always they recall us to the deeper
needs and the greater destinies; and so they try to save us
from the shallow, the slick, the facile, the cruel, and to
show us that the world of men is not meant to be a
battlefield or a laboratory but a family.

Keep the words of God, the things that God does and
the events and experiences that he sends you, in your
heart; use them in prayer and sacrifice to increase your
vision of the length and breadth and height and depth;
then, no doubt, you will share with Mary in the sorrows
of the seven swords, but you will share with her also in
the motherhood of man. And in the degree to which you
can copy her humility, the humility of her *ecce ancilla
Domini*, to that degree you will share in her glory: you of
your own smaller life and smaller world will be able to say
something approaching the words with which she described her future glory in the world as a whole: Behold
from henceforth all generations shall call me blessed, for
he that is mighty hath done great things in me, and holy
is his name.

III

THE VOCATION OF TEARS

Carry me, Christ, on the Cross, which is salvation for the wanderers, sole rest for the wearied, wherein alone is life for those who die.   St. Ambrose

As we know from St. Paul, it is an essential part of the christian life that we should make up what is wanting in the sufferings of Christ, in our flesh, for his body which is the Church; and we have already seen how Pope Pius XII, in *Mystici Corporis*, explains the way in which the Head needs the members for the fulfilment of his work: not that there is any lack of power in him, but that it is his will that the power should reach men through the agency of the Church, so that in fact the salvation of many depends on the prayer and penances which christians offer to God for this intention. And the Pope is at pains to emphasize that this sharing in the redemptive work of Christ as his instruments is not the prerogative and responsibility simply of the Church's pastors: it is part of the life of every christian and, he says, especially of fathers and mothers of families.

We cannot think adequately of the vocation of woman within the Mystical Body of Christ without thinking of the mystery of vicarious suffering and expiation. It is again inseparable from the idea of christian motherhood. Let us think a little of the saint who has a special place in the Church's life as patroness, under our Lady, of married women and mothers, and who is the great exemplar of the glory of the vocation of tears.

Her married life was not an easy one. She had much to

suffer from her husband Patricius, especially from his violent rages; but her quiet strength and patience compelled him at least to respect her; and in the end her prayers and her personality led him to baptism and to a holy death. That was her first victory of vicarious expiation: the first-fruits of her tears.

But it is for her sorrows over her son Augustine that she is famous, just as it is through them that she won her greatest victory for the Church. Mother and son do indeed present just that contrast between the sexes which we have already been considering: Augustine, headstrong and wayward, ambitious, brilliant, making a career for himself, reasoning brilliantly but often wrongheaded; Monica, quiet, constant in her love, humbly standing in the background, following him where his ambition led him so as to be at hand, if occasion offered, to help him, keeping her own deeper wisdom in her heart, weeping over him but not nagging. Later on, when Augustine was preparing for baptism at Cassiacum, Monica joined in their philosophical discussions and they wondered at her wisdom; but it was not her tongue but her tears that had converted him. The words of a bishop who comforted her in her distress are famous: It cannot be that the child of these tears should perish.

Let us note first of all that we are right to speak of the mystery of redemptive tears. We are not concerned here simply with a natural sensibility; and of course we use the word tears to cover not only the sorrow but the prayers and the sufferings, the expiation, as well. We are concerned with the tears that express a deep feeling of responsibility in the sight of God, that are themselves a prayer and a sacrifice to God, and that are a part of the vocation of christian motherhood because the love of the son who causes them is in itself an aspect of the love of God. It is tears such as these that can be the channel of saving grace; it is the children of tears such as these that cannot perish.

There are always wives or mothers, and more than ever perhaps in these present days, who find themselves in the same position as St. Monica; and the first lesson of her life is for them. It is a message of hope and encouragement: they need not despair because they cannot meet impiety or disbelief with weighty argument or brilliant logic — it is not these things alone, anyway, that change the heart of a man. They need only follow the example of St. Monica in her tears and her prayers; and leave the rest to the mercy of God.

But the lesson has a far wider application than that. Mgr. Bougaud, at the end of his *Life of St. Monica*, thanks her because in revealing her heart to him she has taught him also to know his own: Thanks to thy teaching, he says, I know now better than I did before at what cost souls are to be ransomed, and that if a true mother must possess a priestly heart, the heart of a true priest must be a maternal one.[1] For since it is part of the office of the priest to lead souls back to God, he cannot carry out his work unless he possesses the qualities of soul of a Monica. If he is hard and cold, if he lacks understanding of and sympathy for the struggles and temptations and weaknesses of human beings, he will never be able to do his work, however learned he may be in theology and eloquent in preaching. Some indeed may be kept from the danger of an aloof superiority simply because of their consciousness of their own inability to achieve ordinary rectitude of conduct themselves; but they are not necessarily in better case — a sense of one's own sin is not of much avail unless it is allied with the sense of God and the determination to learn more and more to think and to will with the heart of Christ. And when you have both these

[1] Cf. BUTLER: *Lives of the Saints* (New & Revised Ed.), May 4.

things, when you have both sympathy for your fellow-sinners and identity of will with the will of God, then you have what is required to fulfil the vocation, not only of wives and mothers of families, not only of priests, but of all who are called to share in the priesthood of Christ by a life of redemptive prayer and work and suffering in the world: and in particular, the life of christian womanhood.

Let us think a little more of these two conditions. Augustine, speaking to God of the sorrow of his mother over his sins, and the tears she shed for them, says in the *Confessions*: For she, through that faith and the spirit which thou hast given her, saw my death; and thou didst hearken to her, O Lord. Thou didst hearken to her, and didst not despise her tears when in streams they rolled down her cheeks on the ground wherever she prayed; thou didst hearken to her.

She saw his death: that is the first thing. You cannot do this work if you have only an academic interest in the sins of the world. She saw his death; but she saw it as a death in her own heart; and so God hearkened to her tears. You have to learn to say *De Profundis* for the whole human family, not as something outside yourself but as something identified with yourself. You have therefore to learn first the sense of sin; and that means learning both to love God and to love and understand the world of men. And that in its turn means thinking long and deeply; it means keeping the words of life in your heart; it means, not trying to escape the cruelties and crudities of reality, but on the contrary trying to enfold all the pain of the world in the arms of your pity, and feeling responsible for the sin of men as a mother feels responsible for the sin of her son, and, as Augustine says again of his mother, travailing in birth with them as often as you perceive that they go astray from God.

The second condition is as important as the first.

Monica led Patricius away from his vices and back to God; she did so, Augustine tells us, because she was able to reveal God to him by her virtues, in which God had made her beautiful. If you are to lead men they must feel your understanding and sympathy; but if you are to lead men to God they must sense in you the presence of God. Those tears are redemptive which spring from the heart of Christ within you. They are redemptive in a double sense.

There is first the mystery of vicarious expiation, even in some strange way of vicarious sorrow, in itself. Because the Church is a communion of saints, and a communion of sinners, a true mystical body in which all the members share a common life, it follows that the well-being of the whole body is enhanced by the holiness of individual members; and we have seen already how the prayers and penances of the faithful christian are meant to be the channels whereby the saving grace of Christ comes to those in need. And it is not only that you can expiate the sins of others by prayer and penance: God hearkened to the *tears* of Monica. To bear the weight of the sins of others in your heart, as our Lord bore the sins of the world on the Cross, as the saints bear them because of their oneness with him, that is in itself a sacrifice which has the power to expiate, so that the tears seem themselves to freshen and quicken the arid soil of the world.

That is indeed the second sense in which they are redemptive. It is not only that they can *merit* for another the grace of sorrow and renewal: they themselves can be the *instrument* used by God for its bestowal, a part of the process of conversion. We know how the words of Christ could change the whole heart of a man; perhaps we ought to think more of the power of the tears of Christ to change the heart of the world. He wept over Lazarus in the tomb, and Lazarus was raised to life; and surely it is permissible to see in this scene a symbol of the power of tears to quicken and restore. He wept over Jerusalem; and surely it is right that we should remember it often in these days, when hatred and persecution of the Jewish race has cast so deep a stain on the soul of Europe, and see in it precisely the promise of the final redemption of Israel of which St. Paul speaks. Can it be that the child of these tears should perish? It cannot; because the tears are an offering to God, on behalf of the child, of that sorrow which is the necessary condition of the return to God; it cannot, because the tears themselves may, in God's mercy, be the way in which the heart of the child is softened again and made again receptive, and so prepared for grace.

The tears themselves are redemptive; but they lead beyond themselves, lead to the making up of what is wanting in the *sufferings* of Christ. The Pope, in the encyclical we have already been considering, tells us how Christ proved his love for the Church not only by his labours and prayers but also by his sorrows and sufferings, gladly and lovingly endured for the Church's sake: it was only with his blood that he purchased the Church. And we for our part are to try to do the same. For, he says, although our Lord's passion and death merited for the Church an infinite treasure of grace, yet it is not God's will that these graces should be granted to us all at once; and the measure in which they are bestowed depends in no small part on the way in which we do penance in union with the sufferings of Christ, and accept humbly and gladly as he did the burdens and sorrows which life brings us.

This, then, is practical advice for those who would fulfil the vocation of woman in the world. There is first of all bodily penance: we need not think of anything dramatic, and indeed the only safe rule where physical mortification

is concerned is that it should be done only under the
advice of a confessor; but there are all sorts of small and
secret and in themselves insignificant ways in which the
will can be trained to obedience to God through the
training of the body. Then there is the mortification of
the spirit: here you are on safer ground, for the mortification of the flesh needs to be limited but there is no limit
to the extent to which you can healthily curb idle curio-
sity, ill-temper, criticism of others, and so on. And finally,
and above all, there is the life-long mortification of freely,
gladly, and unconditionally accepting the will of God,
not only at the present moment but for the whole of the
future, no matter what it may bring; and included in this
acceptance is the act of worship which turns all the sorrows
and joys alike into the material of sacrifice, and a sacrifice
which can be for the salvation of many. Included in it
also is the deep christian joy which will be not cast down
by misfortune or failure, and the patience which, where
the saving of the world is concerned, will never give in,
and the love which will never grow tired.

When you look round the world to-day it is easy to
despair. There is so much suffering, so much horror, so
much blank misery; and perhaps some of it touches you
very closely; and you feel that your own suffering because
of it is useless and helpless, and so there is no hint of hope
in your heart that out of it all some good may come. You
must not think that. You must remember Monica and the
vocation of tears. You must remember how the Pope, as
he writes of the endless throng of suffering human beings
passing before his eyes, bids them lift up their eyes in
confidence to heaven. Let them all remember, he says,
that their sufferings are not in vain; they will be great
gain to them, and to the Church, if only they take courage
and bear them patiently with that end in view. You need
not be desperate because you can do nothing to help the

millions who have been overwhelmed by misery, because
you can do nothing to stop the crimes and brutalities, the
seemingly irremediable evils, which are being wrought in
the world to-day. By the fact that you suffer for them
before God, and offer your suffering for them to God, you
are already redeeming them. Out of evil good can come:
the condition is the shedding of redemptive tears.

Even apart from the special horrors and sins which the
war has brought in its train, the world of to-day stands in
urgent need of the tears of the lovers of God. It needs
them precisely because of its lack of the sense of depth,
of the sense of sin, of the sense of its need of God and its
need of redemption. If you are willing to work and pray
and suffer in order to restore to the world its sense of these
things, then you are accepting a vocation the importance of
which you cannot exaggerate. Without this we are lost.
Without this we may have grandiose schemes of social
betterment, we may achieve the abolition of many social
evils and the distribution of many social benefits; we may
be given a vast increase in material comforts; we may
even find ourselves witnessing a renaissance of culture;
but they will all be only in the end a distraction, and
only in the end turn to ashes in our mouths, unless first
of all we learn to cry to God out of the depths. They will
be a distraction as the progress made by scientific humanism has in fact been a distraction in the past: they will
make the surface of life more comfortable and more
pleasing, and so we shall forget that the realities of life
are escaping us. We shall forget in particular the under-
ground world; or we shall do our best not to think of it;
and so we shall still be modern man in search of a soul —
unconsciously searching, consciously trying to pretend
there is nothing to search for; and then in the end once
again the underworld will break forth and we shall be
powerless to control it, and there will be more chaos and

more horror and more misery and more accumulation of evil. . . .

This vocation of tears is not a luxury in the Church's life. There are vocations which bring it great blessings and enrich its life but which it could no doubt do without. This is not one of them. If it had not been for the tears of Monica the Church would have no St. Augustine: the whole world to-day is an Augustine, waiting for the redemptive tears which will bring upon it the grace of God and restore it to life in him.

There is a prayer in the missal which begs for the gift of tears: it is a grace we all need for ourselves, and we ought to ask for it. But you who have this work to do in the world, you need to ask for it with special urgency. Augustine, when he is describing how he tricked his mother and set out secretly for Rome, speaks of her as with sorrow seeking what with sorrow she had brought forth. Constantly he reverts to the idea of her double motherhood: she brought him forth, he says, both in her flesh, that he might be born into this temporal light, and in her heart, that he might be born into the light eternal; and as it was through the pains of childbirth that she brought him into the world of time, so it was through the agony of her sorrow for his sins and her fears for his soul that she brought him forth again into the life of eternity. She brought him forth again in her heart; if you are to do the work she did, either for particular human beings or for the world of man as a whole, you must have a heart like hers.

But this comparison between the birth in the flesh and the birth in the spirit leads us on to think of another aspect, and an essential aspect, of the vocation of tears. You remember the words of our Lord: A woman when she is in labour hath sorrow because her hour is come; but when she hath brought forth the child she remembereth no more the anguish, for joy that a man is born into the world. And you remember that our Lord uses this as an illustration of what he has just said to his disciples about themselves: Amen, amen, I say to you . . . you shall be made sorrowful, but your sorrow shall be turned into joy. The sorrow we have been thinking of so far has to be set beside that joy which is an essential quality of the true christian, if it is to be seen aright. Compare, in the *Confessions*, the grief of Augustine over his mother's death with his earlier grief over his friend. When his friend dies he is plunged into despair: I became a great puzzle to myself, he says, and I asked my soul why it was so sad and why so disquieted within me; and it knew not what to answer. And if I said, Trust thou in God, it rightly did not obey; for that dearest one whom it had lost was both truer and better than that phantasm in which it was bidden to trust. But when his mother dies his sorrow is not unrelieved bitterness, for in the meantime he has found God in his heart; and so, it was a comfort to me, he says to God, to weep in thy sight, concerning her and for myself, concerning myself and for her. And he is not compelled, as he was in the former case, to try to forget the sorrow by seeking for new joys; the sorrow itself is gradually turned into joy. There is indeed in the human heart a strange power of housing joy and sorrow together; and you find it very clearly in the saints, who seem most gay and untroubled when they are suffering most. You find it in one of those small revealing touches with which Augustine paints for us his mother's personality: when he says that to the women who complained to her of the violent treatment they suffered at the hands of their husbands she gave grave advice but gave it — as if in jest.

Your sorrow shall be turned into joy. We should compare this saying of our Lord's again with another one: And when you fast, be not as the hypocrites, sad. You

I have to *believe,* first of all, that out of all the evil good will eventually come; secondly, you have to believe that your tears, if they are shed in God's sight, will themselves help to bring forth the good from the evil; thirdly, therefore, you have to be glad and gay even in your sorrow, because your sorrow is such that God will incline his ear to it and turn it into joy — and turn it into joy by bringing joy and rest to those for whom you sorrow.

And as joy is an essential part of the christian life, so it is in particular an essential part of the vocation of tears, not only because in the sorrow there is always the joy of hope, but because if the sorrow turns into gloom it ceases to be redemptive. You cannot offer a sacrifice of praise with sullen lips: if you are going to offer God your tears and penances for the saving of souls you must first of all have the faith and hope and love whose joy is never extinguished. Blessed is he who loves thee, and his friend in thee, and his enemy for thee, said Augustine in prayer to God; for he alone loses no one dear to him, to whom all are dear in the One who can never be lost. Blessed, because then he will never despair, but will make his sorrow a sacrifice of praise. And blessed too because his sorrows will fulfil, in the second sense we considered earlier, the vocation of tears: they will themselves bring comfort and light to other hearts because of the joy that goes with them. If Monica had perpetually nagged at her son, if she had been always weeping and wailing in his presence, she would have driven him not to God but to desperation. His mother kept the words in her heart. The tears must be shed in secret, to God; to the world you must show laughter and joy.

Let us return for a moment to family life, and see these ideas there, in their most obvious setting. What we have to keep reminding ourselves of is this: that the vocation of tears is not a highflown romantic fantasy, but part of the ordinary living of an ordinary humdrum life. You find saints who suffer incredible things for the saving of the world, yes; but these are the exceptions. What you have to try to imitate is not their extraordinary ways of expiating for the world's sins, but the extraordinary love and joy and singlemindedness with which they bear their crosses. You can perfectly well carry out this vocation to the full by doing nothing more elaborate and alarming than what is provided by the ordinary drudgery of kitchen and nursery. You can also carry it out by accepting without gloom and despondency the inevitable evolution of married life precisely *from* the romantic glamour of the first days to the less exciting but more important work of building the family in oneness of mind which follows. If you try to cling to the glamour at all costs, and therefore run away from the duties of motherhood and the work of making a home, you miss the realities of life: the glamour will fade despite your efforts and then you will find you have nothing with which to replace it. If on the other hand you accept the fact that the making of a family together implies and effects a change from the early glamour to the later, more pedestrian but deeper, unity of mind and heart, then you will not only not be missing the reality of life, you will also be fulfilling, without fuss but with lasting effect, this vocation we have been considering. You will have your full share of disappointment and discomfort and hard work and self-discipline; but they will stand you and your family in good stead in the day of need, if all the time you live them in the sight of God, and for the love of God, and turn them, and your family through them, into the joy and happiness which are the fruit of living with God.

The same is true in substance of work in the world. It is possible that God wants of you some extraordinary self-dedication; it is far more probable that he wants you only to turn the ordinary everyday troubles and crosses of life into joy. Every form of work has its hardships, its strains and boredoms; every friendship has its problems and its crosses; every day has its incidental vexations. Physical pain, mental worry, the sorrows of the heart: if you take them all as coming from God's hands and force yourself to be merry in spite of them, so that the world knows you for the depth of your understanding and sympathy but also for the constancy of your gaiety, you will be fulfilling your vocation. And quite apart from the debt it owes you indirectly, for the graces you have earned for it, it will be your debtor immediately and directly, because, like Monica, you will bring it peace.

Pray to Monica to obtain for you her own gift of tears, so that like her you may help to make up what is wanting in the sufferings of Christ, in your flesh, for the Church; pray to her to obtain for you the sense of sin and the will to expiate, for only if we have been planted together in the likeness of the death of Christ shall we be also in the likeness of his resurrection. Pray to her that you may learn to say, and help the world to say, *De Profundis*, and to say it with sorrow and yet with hope and with joy because of the Man who is born into the world and in whom all other men may be born again. So you will do glory to God and good to men; for it is only when we have learnt to say *De Profundis* from our hearts that we can merit — and help the world to merit — the grace to say *Gloria in excelsis* and to have what follows from it: to say, Glory to God in the heavens, and to have, on earth, peace.

IV

THE LEADERSHIP OF LOVE.

She shall crush thy head; and thou shalt lie in wait for her heel. (Gen. iii. 15)

To study the life of our Lady or St. Monica is to gain an impression of an influence silent, secret, self-effacing, patient, working in the background. But we shall miss its meaning if we think of it as something passive, or as limited to the task of supporting and sustaining, comforting and encouraging, expiating. It is active and creative: it not only sustains activity, but calls it forth. That is indeed the most obvious fact about woman throughout the course of history: it is her fate to bring out either what is best or what is worst in men. They will perform herculean feats of bravery to win her, or they will cheat and lie and do crimes of violence; they will fight among themselves for her; for her sake they will become wise and strong and gentle, or they will sink into a servility and a degradation which in the end empty them of their manhood. One of the old Greek thinkers spoke of God as being the cause of all things inasmuch as he is that which all things desire and aspire to and are moved to reach out to by their own growth and fulfilment; in something of the same way it is the destiny of woman to lead man to action through the leadership of love. Our Lord said: When I shall be lifted up, I shall draw all things to me. It depends upon the extent to which woman possesses within her, like Catherine, the heart of Christ, whether her summons shall lead men to heaven or to hell. We can see the two possible alternatives very clearly if we look at the contrasting figures of Eve in the story of *Genesis* and Beatrice in the *Comedy* of Dante.

You remember how the story of the fall of man begins: The serpent was more subtle than any of the beasts of the earth which the Lord God had made. The devil is a clever debater, skilled in the art of making argument appear to do service to truth when it is actually masking falsehood; it should have been the prerogative of Eve to answer his parade of reason with her own feminine wisdom. Why hath God commanded you that you should not eat of every tree of paradise? he asks her; and she replies that it is not every tree, it is only one tree that they are forbidden to eat of, or indeed touch, lest they die. You notice the childlike exaggeration: we are not even allowed to touch it, she says, so deeply had the importance of the command of God impressed her. But she was not childlike enough. The symbolism is not of some obvious crime that is forbidden them; but of something in itself indifferent; because it is of the essence of their nature as creatures to acknowledge the power and the right of God to command, to accept the idea that, as Julian of Norwich tells us, God has not only the knowledge which he makes known to us but his secret knowledge also, which none can seek to know. She should have preserved the humility before God which is proper to her wisdom; but the fruit was fair to the eyes and delightful to behold: Your eyes shall be opened and you shall be as gods, the serpent told her; as gods, autonomous, deciding for themselves what shall be good and what shall be evil; her belief in the divine threat is shaken, and her trust in the divine goodness with it: and she took of the fruit and did eat, and gave to her husband who did eat.

She had exercised her influence; but because it was in defiance of her feminine wisdom it was baleful. And their eyes *were* opened, the story goes on, with that irony which in the old testament as in the new seems so often to cloak the sorrow and the pity of God; they perceived themselves to be naked (and indeed they were: conscious of their lost integrity, bereft, cut off from God); and they sewed together fig-leaves and made themselves aprons — no longer a king and queen, but like naughty children ashamed of themselves.

And as the day wore on they heard the Lord God walking in paradise, and they hid themselves, so that God called to Adam and said to him, Where art thou? Hitherto they had walked with him in the evenings: they had been contemplatives, sharing in his life; now they would be able to no longer, they would have to grope for him, as we have to grope for him now. And then Adam tries to put the blame on the woman whom God had given him, and so to put it yet further back, on God himself. And Eve in her turn says that the serpent deceived her: as indeed he had deceived her with his forensic guile, when she should have been listening to the voice of her own God-given wisdom. And then, finally, there comes the judgment, the sorrows that will be multiplied for the woman; but there comes also the promise and the hope: I will put enmities between thee and the woman, he says to the serpent, and thy seed and her seed: she shall crush thy head, and thou shalt lie in wait for her heel.

We have been thinking of Monica as the woman who brought forth her son, first in the flesh, into the light of this material world, and then in her heart, into the light eternal; and we have been thinking of the way in which all women are meant to share in the work of bringing back souls to God, to re-birth in the light eternal, through their prayers and their tears. The *Genesis* story takes us a step further. The mission of woman is not merely a passive, an expiatory one: it is the active mission of the leadership of love. The words of God to the serpent carry in them the promise of the Word made flesh; and as Mary is to bring forth the Son who shall crush the serpent's head (so that it makes little difference whether we read, with the Vulgate, *she* shall crush thy head, or with other manuscripts, *it*, the seed which is Christ, shall crush thy head), so it is the destiny of all who share in her vocation of spiritual motherhood to bring forth in their hearts those who will share in her Son's battle against evil. (It is the destiny of woman to form man, by her active leadership, into the likeness of Christ, to help him to return to the source of life, and knowledge, and power: in other words, to reverse the primal sin, to reject the creature's attempt to be as a god, to recognize the limitations of human reason, and the true emancipation of the human will which is obedience to God. It is her destiny to show man, by being herself God's handmaid, how to rise to the fullness of his stature: how to accept the destiny of shared divinity which is offered him by humbly accepting the essential powerlessness of the humanity which is his natural state.

How is she to do all this? By the twofold office of love: by teaching; and by empowering, encouraging, drawing onwards to life.

This twofold office we shall see fulfilled in the figure of Beatrice. We shall see it there in its clearest and most cogent form; but we must not narrow down to a particular type of relationship what is of itself a universal vocation. The story of Dante and Beatrice corresponds and contrasts with the story of Adam and Eve, the world's first lovers; and applies most immediately to other lovers; but it has its general application, and we shall come to it later on. Let us first of all think over the story itself.

She too, like Eve, is in the earthly paradise when we first meet her, and when Dante first meets her again, in the *Divine Comedy*. And let us notice the stages of their meeting;

for first of all it is not by sight that he realizes her presence
but

> *Per occulta virtù, che da lei mosse,*
> *D'antico amor sentì la gran potenza,*

by a hidden influence which proceeded from her he was
conscious of the mighty power of his early love. And then,
when she bids him look at her —

> *Guardami ben: ben son, ben son Beatrice,*

Look well, I am, I am indeed Beatrice — he is filled with
overwhelming shame.

> *Così la madre al figlio par superba,*
> *Com' ella parve a me; perchè d'amaro*
> *Sente 'l sapor della pietade acerba:*

she seemed to him as commanding as a mother appears to
her son, for there is a bitterness in the flavour of severe pity.
As commanding as a mother: we misunderstand love
completely and degrade it if we confuse it with a soft
sentimentality. Love is what seeks the good of the one
loved; and sometimes that must imply severity. Beatrice
in fact rebukes him roundly — she makes him cry. She
rebukes him for having deserted her:

> *Alcun tempo 'l sostenni col mio volto;*
> *Mostrando gli occhi giovinetti a lui,*
> *Meco 'l menava in dritta parte vôlto:*

for a time she had sustained him by her countenance; by
displaying her youthful eyes to him she led him with her
in the right way. But when she was twenty-five she died;
and he, forsaking her memory, had given his heart to
another. We do not know who this other girl was; as a
symbol she has been taken by commentators to mean
philosophy as opposed to theology; we might say rather,
reason as spoilt and diminished by its attempt to be

autonomous as against the wisdom which is the gift of God, for as a symbol it is from the primal sin that she seeks to recall us. And she goes on to say how all her efforts to save him, all her communications, were of no avail, and there was only one thing left to do: to show him the lost people. Either the pride of reason independent of God must be allowed to go on until it destroys all that it has built, so that then the soul may realize where its true greatness lies; or else it must be shown how it *will* in fact inevitably destroy itself, by being shown the lost people, the people who have come to the tragic end of the process and are fixed, by their own will, in destruction. Then, if the journey through the *Inferno* has had its effect, if the exploration of the deep underworld and what it reveals of sunken humanity has opened the soul once again to the sense of depth and of the need of redemption, so that it can cry for the mercy of God and the grace of re-birth, then it is possible, and it is time, for Beatrice to begin the second part of her mission, to reveal to him something of the life and the nature of God.

And how is this to be accomplished? You remember the song that was sung by the three ladies as they came forward dancing:

> *Volgi, Beatrice, volgi gli occhi santi,*
> *Era la lor canzone, al tuo fedele,*
> *Che per vederti ha mossi passi tanti:*

Turn, Beatrice, turn your eyes to your faithful one, who has journeyed so far to have sight of you. And they beg her also to unveil her face, and reveal her smile to him. But he for his part has already told us how

> *Mille disiri più che fiamma caldi*
> *Strinsermi gli occhi agli occhi rilucenti:*

a thousand longings, hotter than flame, fixed his eyes upon

her radiant eyes; but they were steadfastly fixed upon the Gryphon, Christ, alone; and in them, like the sun reflected in a glass, it was the Gryphon that he saw. And when she has obeyed the behest of the three ladies and revealed her holy smile,[1] and he is so rapt in gazing that his other senses are as though in abeyance, still she will not let him deny her true nature and his by idolatry: it is to the Gryphon that she is to lead him. So, later, she tells him:

Al carro tieni or gli occhi:

Fix now your eyes upon the chariot; and he, the willing slave of her commandments, does as she bids him.

A thousand longings fixed his eyes upon her radiant eyes — but they were steadfastly fixed upon the Gryphon. That is the central point, the essence of the leadership of love. She is not to be merely that *through* which God is revealed: she is also to be that *in* which God is revealed. To fulfil her office she must have the gift of kindling and keeping his love; but she must herself be filled with the sight of God — not to forget him but to lead him with her. So she reverses the thing that Eve had done: she reverses the primal sin, and in doing so she reverses the effect of it upon man. It is not without good reason that the poet, as he goes on to describe the procession through the forest, reminds us that it was uninhabited because of the sin of her who had trusted the serpent; and later they come to the tree whose boughs are bare of leaf and flower, the tree of knowledge of good and evil, and they praise the Gryphon because he has not plucked anything from it; and then finally the tree itself is renewed as the Gryphon ties to it the chariot-pole which represents the Cross — the wood on which the rebellion of Adam was wiped out by the perfect self-dedication of man, in the person of the Son, to God.

[1] Dante's word is *riso*: more accurately a laugh.

The first office of love in its leadership is to teach. But
its essential method of teaching is not to expound, to
reason, to demonstrate to the mind; it is to reveal to the
heart of the lover the truth as incarnate in the object loved.
If you see the truth coldly and objectively stated it may
fail to compel you; if you see it shining in the eyes you love
it will become, like them, a part of yourself. It is the prerogative of love that it can cause the truth to become in
this way identified with what is loved; so that then the
truth itself is seen in a new way; it becomes, as theologians
say, *connatural*, possessed, realized as part of the felt
oneness of the two who love — no longer merely the
material of a cold intellectual judgment, but something
which immediately draws the heart. St. Paul speaks of the
difficulty of loving the God whom we cannot see, as
compared with the created beauty which we can see: it is
the privilege and the responsibility of Beatrice to reveal
the invisible to man, so ready to become immersed in the
visible and the material. That is why she is given the
privilege of her wisdom and her power. But it is not only
a privilege but a hard responsibility, because it is so easy
on earth to misuse the power: it is so easy for the woman
to fail to keep her eyes fixed steadfastly on the Gryphon,
so that when the man gazes at them he sees not God but
only herself. Eve had the power; and she used it wrongly
because she herself was led astray after a supposed independence of judgment and will which was in direct
contradiction to her nature. Beatrice had the power; but
she used it to redeem and lead back to God, because she
herself loved God above all things, and all things in God.
So, as the handmaid of the Mediator, she mediates in her
turn: she draws man to know and love her that she may
then lead him beyond herself to that Beauty of which she
and all things else are but a pale and partial reflection;
she leads him to the Cross; and when he in his turn goes

back to the world to work in it for the fulfilling of the redemptive purposes of Christ, she is in his work and the glory of it, for it is she who has made it possible by bringing him forth in her heart into the eternal light.

But love not only teaches; it spurs to action; it leads. Beatrice does more than cause Dante to gaze on Christ:

Al carro tieni or gli occhi; e, quel che vedi,
Ritornato di là, fa' che tu scrive:

Fix your eyes now, she says, upon the chariot; and what you see, be sure you write it when you return to earth. It is not a command which he will find difficult or distasteful to carry out: there could hardly be a greater incentive to write than to be told to write by love. Love, like wisdom, reaches from end to end mightily, but disposes all things sweetly; fear or force can produce action by compulsion, forcing on as it were from behind; but love produces action by a free and glad impulsion, drawing onwards from in front. It is because Dante is led by his love to understand something of infinite Love, and so to be in a state of love towards all men, that he is impelled in all his actions to spread through the world the spirit of that Love, the spirit of Christ the Saviour: as long as the influence remains with him, all his actions are coloured, informed, by the charity which possesses him, and so become healing and saving for the souls of men.

That is what love's leadership can do in its twofold office. By leading her lover to God as revealed in herself she gives him the sense of his ultimate destiny and direction; she gives him a sense of men's brotherhood in God; she gives him a glimpse of the immensities of the destiny offered him, the heights he is to scale, the heaven which awaits him; she gives him, in his own shame, a sense of his own blindness and stupidity, and therefore prepares him for the grace of humility and patience and the power to learn. In other words, she gives him the sense of the length and breadth and height and depth; and when he has once been given that he can begin to live, to accept and exult in the grace and the stature of the sons of God. So Beatrice fulfils the destiny for which she was given her *occhi rilucenti*, her radiant eyes: he sees her gazing like an eagle at the Sun, and is therefore impelled to do the same; and when, unable any longer to endure the light, he withdraws his eyes from It, it is only to fix them upon hers, and to find himself changed by looking, as Glaucus the fisherman was changed by eating of the divine herb at the shore's edge and became himself a sea-god. Higher and higher he climbs, led onward by her eyes and her smile, till at last he can gaze even on the blinding glory of the light inaccessible of the Godhead; and so his journey ends, in the

Luce eterna, che sola in te sidi:

the eternal Light that alone abides within itself, alone knows itself, and, known and knowing, loves and smiles; and her journey, her mission, is ended too:

Quella che imparadisa la mia mente:

she who has thus imparadised his spirit: she has brought him forth in her heart into the light eternal, and his love for her is complete and full at last because at last it is caught up into the still, wordless wonder and joy of the

Amor che muove il Sole e l'altre stelle:

the Love which moves the sun and the other stars.

The story of Dante and Beatrice has its first and most obvious application in the everyday married life of men and women. You do not rob the leadership of love of its substance or its importance by taking away something of the poetry and glamour with which the *Divine Comedy*

presents it. On the contrary. You misunderstand it completely if you suppose that its validity is confined to the
glamorous honeymoon stage of married life; just as you
misunderstand love completely if you suppose that it
passes with the passing of the first romantic idyll — it
should be just beginning. And as the real substance of love
begins only as the real and deep unity of mind and heart
begins, so it may be with love's leadership; for it is a life-
work, and as it never ceases to be necessary, so it need
never cease to exercise its power, however much the
quality of the power itself may change. And the effect of
the power may in fact become greater rather than less as
life goes on and becomes more pedestrian; for passion can
make a man a willing slave but a blind one: so that he
obeys because he loves but without conviction, without
seeing and loving the truth in the eyes he loves and obey-
ing that. As the wife becomes the mother, and gives herself to the second stage of her vocation, she is right, of
course, in preserving the substance of the first, and in
expecting of the man that he will preserve it too, will
continue to regard her, as before, as a lover; but the fact
that he sees in her now in addition the commanding
stature, not of a goddess remote upon her pedestal, but,
as Dante saw Beatrice, of a mother, should mean that
what he learns from her will be far more clearly seen in
itself and therefore far less ephemeral, far less entangled
with the self-regardingness of his passion, and therefore
far more purely divine.

What must she do? She must first of all be herself a
contemplative: she must learn how to look upon the Sun.
Then she must learn the vocation of tears: she must learn
how to sympathize, to co-suffer, she must learn how to
have pity and how to comfort and sustain. But she must
learn also to be strong enough to have, like Beatrice, the
kind of compassion in which there is also a taste of

severity; resisting the temptation to do his will when it is stupid or sinful even though he think her refusal a denial of love. And as her prayer and her pain and her joys and her labours teach her the wisdom which is divine, so that in her eyes there begins to shine the reflection of the eternal light, so she will teach him to turn to her not as to a rival of God or of the work which God would have him do, but as the one who will empower him for his work and help him to do it wisely and humbly in the sight of God; and she will labour, as Monica did in her life with Patricius, not in impatient distress at the difficulties and failures of every day, but with her eyes on the distant horizon, on the end of the journey when at last she will have imparadised his heart.

Let us turn to the wider application of these themes. Whatever your life and your work in the world, they are valid for you. For the condition of the world is determined by the interplay of the spiritual influences which at any given time characterize it, and in the last resort by the one which preponderates. A society in which the vast majority hold that science is all, and suit their actions and ambitions to their belief, will be a world both governed and circumscribed by scientific standards. A society in which the vast majority believe in the *mystique de la force,* the idea that might is in itself something divine, will be a world in which savagery is the accepted weapon of achievement and political self-glorification the only aim. We have known a world determined very largely by the ambitions of scientific humanism on the one hand and the assumption of individualism on the other; the aim an ever-increasing measure of comfort, efficiency and speed; the assumption that each man must fend for himself and look to his own advancement. And latterly we have witnessed, in some parts of our world, a movement of reaction to these ways of thought; but a reaction, alas, whereby these

devils have only been replaced by others worse than themselves. Belief in scientific reason has given way to a
woolly pseudo-mysticism, which at best is the easy prey of
delusions and at worst is no more than a subrational and
fanatic devotion to a personification of the might of the
herd. Individualism has been replaced by a sense of
unity; but a unity in which the individual is submerged
and the personality destroyed. It is not thus that the
world can be saved. The essential need of the west, even
judging by the narrowest human and natural standards,
is an evolution of thought which will preserve the hard-
won values of individual personality while at the same
time restoring the sense of community; so that there may
emerge a society which is neither a simple aggregate of
individuals nor a blind and unselfconscious herd, but a
family. But to say this is to say that the essential need of
the west is the restoration of those qualities of the vocation
of woman which we have been considering. And we who
believe that the first and greatest need of every society is
the need of God, and that its ultimate aim is the building
of a life which can be a preparation for God, can see how
immense and how urgent the same need is. For without
these qualities in our life we miss the one thing necessary,
and all other achievements are but straw: unless God
build the house, they labour in vain that build it.

The same essential responsibility rests upon you, the
same opportunity is open to you, whatever your life and
your work in the world. You cannot live in the world at all
without influencing it to some extent, for better or for
worse. Your immediate influence may be confined to a
small group with whom you share your work or your
leisure hours; and you may be one of those quiet and
retiring people who outwardly seem to exercise no influence on others at all. But you influence others by what
you are much more than by what you do or say; and

though they may be few they influence others in their turn. If you are fulfilling your vocation within yourself you need not be anxious about its effect in the world. God may call you to important active work, or he may want you to live in retirement and solitude; in either case your essential task remains the same: to make sure you are becoming the sort of person he would have you be. You have to become a contemplative, and learn to look upon the Sun. You have to learn, through prayer and detach-ment and the slow growth of wisdom, to love the world aright, in God, and to acquire the hunger and thirst after justice which will make you want to serve it. You have to fulfil in your heart the vocation of tears, learning to have within you the heart of Christ and therefore the compas-sion of Christ. And then, if you are doing all these things, you need not worry about their utility to the world you have learnt to love: for if God does not send you out into the world you will find that the world will begin to come, little by little, to you; no doubt it will not flock to you in any dramatic way, but some will seek you out in the small unnoticed way in which they have sought out some of the saints — and in them, as you know, in the end, when history looks back upon them, it sees one of the forces which have shaped the spirit of their age.

They will begin to look to you, if you have learnt all these things, not only for understanding and sympathy, but for the wisdom which can inspire and lead. They will look to you as to a mediator, who can show them the things of God in terms of the life of man. They will begin to see in you, whatever your way of life, something of the commanding stature of motherhood, and something of the beauty of holy living wherewith God has made you beautiful. You will speak to them, even though you are silent, of things of which perhaps they would otherwise have never thought, but which they may come to realize

as the pearl of great price, the search for which makes all
other ambitions, by comparison, insignificant. You will
reveal to them, and through them to the world, something
of the length and breadth and height and depth; and so
you will have your share in the redemptive work of Christ;
you will have your share in restoring to the world the
deep wisdom it has lost, and therefore the unity towards
which it ineffectually strives, and therefore, finally, the
peace for which it longs.

If there are enough in the world to accept the vocation
of woman, and really to *fulfil* it, it is they who will save
from ruin and turn to good the social ambitions, the
political plannings, the reasoned search for a reasonable
world-order, which are the work of man. That work is of
course necessary for the world; just as the work of the
husband is necessary to the family. We have been concerned in these meditations only with the vocation of
woman; and perhaps sometimes it has appeared as though
the man had little of his own to contribute to the life of the
family and the world. That would be an absurd distortion
of the truth. A man may in fact contribute nothing but
folly; but then so may a woman. We are concerned here
with what ought to be. The man and the woman have
each an essential contribution to make; and it is an essen-
tially different contribution. The man has to teach in his
turn, he has to lead to God, he has to bear sorrows and
responsibilities; but all these things he has to do in a
different way, the way of practical reason and judgment,
of reasoned initiative, the way of the wisdom of a masculine
mind which even in an Augustine or a John of the Cross
is never quite the same as the wisdom which is born in a
woman's heart. The safety and salvation of the world
depend on the combined work of man and woman alike;
if either fails the world must fail; but it remains true that
we in this age have been living under a system in which

the masculine mind predominates; and we desperately need the fullness of the vocation of woman.

She shall crush the head of the serpent. Pray to Mary and to the other saints who have carried out so completely and so gloriously the work of woman: pray to them first to obtain for you their humility and their readiness to be taught by God, that so you may come to share in their wisdom and patience and strength and power. Learn to say with Mary, Behold the handmaid of the Lord; and then you will have also a part in the saving of the generations that are with you and the generations that are yet to come; you will be able to say with something of her pride and her humility something resembling her *magnificat*, for he that is mighty will have done great things in you and through you, and in you and through you his name will be magnified; and however apparently unromantic your life, you will be able to say with Beatrice, *Guardami ben'*, Look well at me, for I am the one of whom the song was sung by those about the chariot: *Benedicta qui venit in nomine Domini*, Blessed who cometh in the name of the Lord. And the generations of man will call you blessed because in you the mission of Beatrice will have been again fulfilled: the wisdom of your eyes and the pity and gaiety of your smile will have led them to the splendours of the Light inaccessible — your eyes because within them they will have learnt to look upon the image of the Gryphon, and your smile because they will have learnt to realize that the lips are the lips of a woman, but the smile is the smile of Christ.

DATE DUE

AUG 2 '63			
DE 19 '63			
FEB 6 '64			
MR 23 '64			
JA 22 '65			
MR 4 '65			
MR 29 '65			
MY 18 '65			
MY 26 '65			
GAYLORD			PRINTED IN U.S.A.